Contents

Introduction 3
Guide to your A Level Paper 3 exam (Issues and options in psychology) 4
How to use this Exam Workbook 5
Types of A Level exam question 6
The way your answers are marked 7

Classification of schizophrenia 8
Reliability and validity in diagnosis and classification 10
Biological explanations for schizophrenia 15
Psychological explanations for schizophrenia 19
Drug therapy 23
Cognitive behavioural therapy 28
Family therapy 32
Token economy and the management of schizophrenia 37
An interactionist approach 41

Introduction

The Complete Companions series of psychology textbooks were originally devised to provide everything that students would need to do well in their exams. Having produced *The Complete Companion Student Books*, the *Mini Companions*, and the *Revision and Exam Companions*, the next logical step was to produce a series of *Exam Workbooks* to provide a more hands-on experience for psychology students throughout their course and particularly in the period leading up to the exam.

Each of the *Exam Workbooks* in this series is focused on one particular exam. This book covers the topic of Schizophrenia (Paper 3: Section C). Each two-page spread of psychology in the Student Book has an equivalent set of exam questions and advice in this Exam Workbook. It is designed for you to write in, so that you gain valuable experience of constructing responses to a range of different exam questions.

A distinctive feature of this *Exam Workbook* is the 'scaffolding' that we provide to help you produce effective exam answers. The concept of scaffolding is borrowed from the field of developmental psychology, where it is a metaphor describing the role of more knowledgeable individuals in guiding children's learning and development. Our scaffolding takes the form of providing sentence starters and exam tips for most questions, to help you develop the skill of writing effective exam answers. All of the material used in our scaffolding comes from the Student Book, and you are provided with page references for that book so that you can find the right material to complete the answer.

Guide to your A Level Paper 3 exam (Issues and options in psychology)

This paper contains four sections, each worth 24 marks. Section A is compulsory. For Sections B–D, you choose one topic (e.g. for Section C you choose either Schizophrenia or Eating behaviour or Stress) and answer all the questions on that particular topic.

The content of the four sections is as below:

Section A
Issues and debates in psychology

All questions in this section are compulsory. Questions may focus on any of the Issues detailed in the specification (e.g. gender and cultural bias, ethical issues) or Debates (e.g. free will and determinism, the nature-nurture debate, holism and reductionism). There will be a mixture of low (e.g. 1, 2, 3 marks) and high tariff (e.g. 8, 16) marks and also a mixture of AO1 (selection, description), AO2 (application) and AO3 (evaluation) questions. Not all topics will appear in the exam but you need to revise them all as they are all equally likely to appear.

Section B
Relationships; Gender; Cognition and development

You (or more probably your teacher) will have chosen one of these topics to study. Questions can be set on any of the different aspects of these topics that are detailed in the specification (e.g. for 'Relationships', questions might focus on evolutionary explanations for partner preferences, virtual relationships in social media, parasocial relationships etc.). There will be a mix of low and high tariff marks and a mixture of AO1, AO2 and AO3 questions.

Section C
Schizophrenia; Eating behaviour; Stress

In this Section, you have chosen to study schizophrenia. Questions can be set on any of the different aspects of schizophrenia that are detailed in the specification for this topic (e.g. questions might focus on the classification of schizophrenia, biological and psychological explanations, token economies in the treatment of schizophrenia etc.). As with Sections A and B, there will be a mix of low and high tariff marks and a mixture of AO1, AO2 and AO3 questions.

Section D
Aggression; Forensic psychology; Addiction

As with Sections B and C, you will have chosen one of these topics to study. Again, there will be a mix of low and high tariff marks and a mixture of AO1, AO2 and AO3 questions.

The total mark for this paper will be 96 marks and you will have two hours to answer four questions (one from each Section).

Psychology A Level Paper 3

Schizophrenia

The Complete Companion Exam Workbook

for AQA

Name

OXFORD

How to use this Exam Workbook

Specification notes
Each spread begins with the AQA specification entry for this particular topic. This tells you what you need to learn and drives the questions that might be asked in your exam.

Student Book page reference
Each spread has a reminder of the pages where you can read about this topic in **The Complete Companion Year 2 Student Book**.

Scaffolding
Most questions include some 'scaffolding' to help you construct an effective response to the question. This takes the form of sentence starters or appropriate links between points. You can then flesh out this material to make a full answer.

Sample answers
In some topics you will find an answer already provided. This gives you some idea of the appropriate level and length of response necessary to gain full marks.

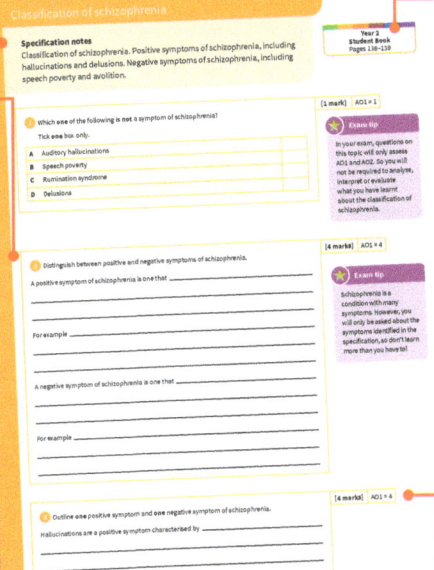
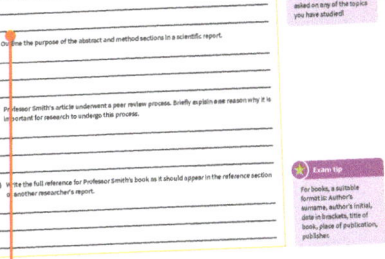

Mark box
Exam questions have different mark 'tariffs'. We have given you an appropriate number of lines in which you can fit your answer. Questions may also be AO1 (description), AO2 (application), or AO3 (evaluation), which will indicate what particular approach you should take in your response.

Questions
Each spread contains sample exam questions. This is not an exhaustive list of all the possible questions you could be asked on this topic, but it gives you the opportunity to practise answering the most common.

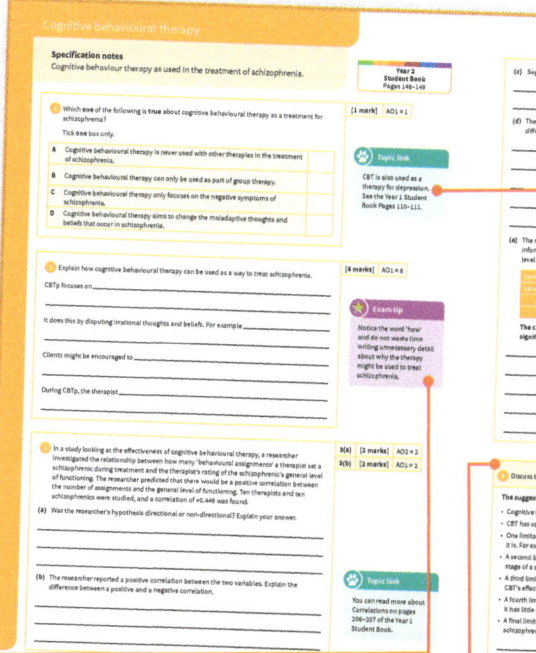
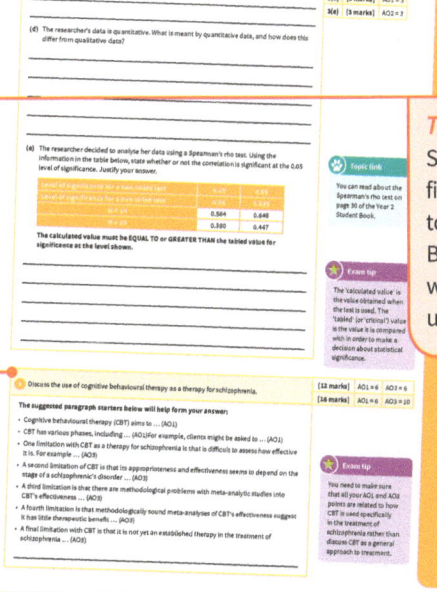

Topic links
Sometimes you will find a link between a topic and the Student Book that we feel will enhance your understanding.

Exam tips
There are helpful exam tips throughout the Exam Workbook. These are general pieces of advice (e.g. the importance of elaborating AO3 points for maximum impact), specific guidance about how to answer a particular question, or how to avoid common mistakes when answering that question.

Essay question
Where appropriate, we have included an extended writing question. We have also included some suggested paragraph starters for the AO1 and AO3 components.

Types of A Level exam question

Question type	Example	Advice
Simple selection/recognition	Which one of the following best describes compliance? (1 mark) A Going along with the majority because we accept their view. B Going along with the majority to gain their approval or avoid their disapproval. C Going along with the majority even though we disagree with their view.	Questions such as these should be straightforward enough, so the trick is making sure you have selected the right answer to gain maximum marks. If you aren't sure which answer is the right one, try crossing through those that are obviously wrong, thus narrowing down your options.
Description questions (e.g. Describe, Outline, Identify, and Name)	Briefly outline the role of the central executive and the episodic buffer in the working memory model. (4 marks)	To judge how much to write in response to a question, simply look at the number of marks available and allow about 25 words per mark. If the sole command word is 'Name' or 'Identify', there is no need to develop a 25 word per mark response, simply identifying or naming (as required by the question) is enough.
Differences/Distinguish between	Distinguish between an insecure–avoidant and insecure–resistant attachment. (4 marks)	You might be tempted to ignore the instruction to 'distinguish between' and simply outline the two terms or concepts named in the question. This is not what is required, and would not gain credit. Words such as 'whereas' and 'however' are good linking words to illustrate a difference between two things.
Applying knowledge	Simon had just returned from a motoring holiday in France, and had spent a fortnight driving on the right hand side of the road. As he drove his car off the ferry, he saw a sign saying 'Remember to drive on the left hand side of the road.' Using your knowledge of interference theory, explain why this sign might be helpful to people like Simon, who are returning to England after driving in France. (4 marks)	In these AO2 questions, you will be provided with a scenario (the question 'stem') and asked to use your psychological knowledge to provide an informed answer. You must make sure that your answer contains not only appropriate psychological content, but that this is set explicitly within the context outlined in the question stem.
Research methods questions	You will be given a description of a study and then a number of short questions such as: (a) Explain the difference between correlations and experiments. (2 marks) (b) Identify a suitable graphical display the researcher could have used, and briefly explain why this display would be appropriate. (2 marks)	Most research methods questions are set within the context of a hypothetical research study. This means that your answers must also be set within the context of that study. If you don't set your answers within the specific context of the study, you cannot receive full marks.
Maths questions	(a) Calculate the percentage of 'thieves' diagnosed as 'affectionless psychopaths'. Show your calculations. (2 marks)	'Maths' questions can appear anywhere on the paper, and can assess your ability to carry out simple calculations, construct graphs, and interpret data, e.g. in this question, a correct answer and appropriate working are necessary for maximum marks.
Evaluation questions	Evaluate the 'failure to function adequately' definition of abnormality. (4 marks)	It is important that you elaborate your evaluative points for maximum marks. We have shown you how to achieve this through the 'scaffolding' feature.
Mixed description and evaluation questions	Outline the use of the cognitive interview and give one limitation of this approach. (6 marks)	Not all questions are straightforward 'description only' or 'evaluation only', but may be mixed. As a rule of thumb, in questions like these you should divide your AO1 and AO3 content equally.
Extended writing questions	Describe and evaluate the 'statistical infrequency' definition of abnormality. (8 marks) Discuss the role of social influence processes in social change. (16 marks)	As a rough guide, 200 words would be appropriate for an answer to an 8-mark question. For a 16 mark question between 400–500 words would be appropriate.
Extended writing questions with specific instructions	Thomas has a phobia of clowns. He relates this to a scary experience he had as a child. He was at the circus when a clown jumped up from the row behind Thomas and startled him so much that his parents had to leave before the show ended. Thomas was so disturbed that he has not even been able to look at a picture of a clown since, let alone go anywhere near one. Describe and evaluate the two-process model as an explanation of phobias. Refer to the example of Thomas as part of your answer. (16 marks)	Some extended writing questions not only require a discussion of a particular theory, model, etc. (i.e. AO1 and AO3), but also have an additional requirement. This example requires you to discuss not only the two-process model of phobias but to do this in the context of the stimulus material provided. Although the model is the key requirement of the question, don't make the mistake of assuming that the applied aspect of the question is less important.

The way your answers are marked

Questions and mark schemes

Examiners mark your answers using mark schemes and marking criteria. These vary from question to question, depending on the specific demands, but below are some examples.

1-mark questions: 1 mark is given for an accurate selection of the right answer or an appropriate identification. Giving the wrong answer or selecting more than one alternative from those available would result in 0 marks.

2-mark questions: For questions such as *'Identify the level of measurement used in this study. Explain your answer'*, 1 mark would be given for identifying the correct level of measurement, and 1 mark for explaining why this is the case. Other 2-mark questions such as *'Calculate the mean score from this data, and show your calculations'* have two requirements (i.e. the correct answer and appropriate workings), which would receive 1 mark each.

3-mark questions: These questions might focus on a descriptive point, e.g. *'Outline one explanation of…'*, where the mark awarded would reflect the detail, accuracy, and overall organisation of your answer. They can also be evaluative, e.g. *'Give one limitation of the statistical infrequency definition of abnormality'*. The number of marks awarded in these AO3 questions is largely determined by the degree of elaboration of your critical point.

4-mark questions: Descriptive and evaluative questions can sometimes be assigned 4 marks, so will require slightly more detail or elaboration than you would write for a 3-mark question. It is useful to try to write the same number of 'points' as the marks available. You may be familiar with the PEEL (Point, Evidence, Explanation, Link) approach that involves making four different statements for a 4-mark AO3 question. Sometimes 4-mark questions are simply two 2-mark questions in disguise, i.e. they contain two specific components, each worth 2 marks.

6-mark questions: These can have very different requirements (e.g. description only, description plus application, or evaluation only), in which case their actual wording varies, e.g. you may come across a question such as *'Describe research into forgetting'* (6 marks) or *'Evaluate Bowlby's maternal deprivation theory'* (6 marks). For each of these you need to decide what is an appropriate level of breadth (how many studies for the first question, how many critical points for the second) and depth (how much detail, how much elaboration). Usually the answer is two, (i.e. describe two studies) as this is a suitable compromise in the need for both breadth and depth in these questions.

8 and 16-mark questions: Questions above 6 marks are generally referred to as 'extended writing' questions. They always have more than one requirement, so examiners will be assessing (usually) both AO1 and AO3 in what is effectively a short essay response. There are four main criteria that an examiner will be looking for in extended writing answers.

Description (AO1) – have you described the material accurately and added appropriate detail? There are a number of ways in which you can add detail. These include expanding your description by going a bit deeper (i.e. giving more information rather than offering a superficial overview), providing an appropriate example to illustrate the point being made, or adding a study (which adds authority and evidence of wider reading).

Evaluation (AO3) – have you used your critical points effectively? Have you elaborated the points you have made? Examiners will be assessing whether you have made the most of a critical point. A simple way is to identify the point (e.g. that there is research support), justify the point (e.g. provide the findings that back up your claim) and elaborate the point (e.g. link back to the thing being evaluated, demonstrate how research support strengthens a theory or adds support to a research study). In this Exam Workbook we have aimed at writing 30 words of evaluation per mark available for AO3.

- 8-mark question = 4 marks for AO3 and so 120 words of evaluation
- 16-mark question = we have worked on the assumption that you would use five AO3 points of 60 words each. However, you might decide to just use four of the AO3 points we provide and expand each to 75 words. This is entirely appropriate.

Organisation – does your answer flow and are your arguments clear and presented in a logical manner? This is where planning pays off as you can organise a structure to your answer before you start writing. This is always more effective than just sticking stuff down as it occurs to you!

Specialist terminology – have you used the right psychological terms (giving evidence that you have actually understood what you have read or been taught) rather than presented your material in lay (i.e. non-specialist) language? This does not mean you have to write in an overly formal manner. Students often mistakenly believe that they have to use the sorts of words that they would never use in everyday life!

How do examiners work out the right mark for an answer?

Mark schemes are broken down into different levels. Each of these levels has a descriptor, which describes what an answer for that level should look like i.e. an average performance for that range of marks. Examiners will first choose the level they think the answer is and then use the 'magnet effect'. This means once they have decided the level, they will decide whether it is closer to the level above (pulling it to the top of that level), closer to the one below (pulling marks to the bottom of the level) or just in the middle.

Answers

All answers for this Exam Workbook can be found at:

www.oxfordsecondary.co.uk/completecompanionsanswers

Classification of schizophrenia

Specification notes
Classification of schizophrenia. Positive symptoms of schizophrenia, including hallucinations and delusions. Negative symptoms of schizophrenia, including speech poverty and avolition.

Year 2 Student Book Pages 138–139

1 Which **one** of the following is **not** a symptom of schizophrenia?

Tick **one** box only.

A	Auditory hallucinations
B	Speech poverty
C	Rumination syndrome
D	Delusions

[1 mark] AO1 = 1

2 Distinguish between positive and negative symptoms of schizophrenia.

A positive symptom of schizophrenia is one that _____

_____

_____

For example _____

_____

_____

A negative symptom of schizophrenia is one that _____

_____

_____

For example _____

_____

_____

[4 marks] AO1 = 4

> ⭐ **Exam tip**
>
> Schizophrenia is a condition with many symptoms. However, you will only be asked about the symptoms identified in the specification, so don't learn more than you have to!

3 Outline **one** positive symptom and **one** negative symptom of schizophrenia.

Hallucinations are a positive symptom characterised by _____

_____

_____

Avolition is a negative symptom characterised by _____

_____

_____

_____

[4 marks] AO1 = 4

> ⭐ **Exam tip**
>
> In your exam, questions on this topic will only assess AO1 and AO2. So you will not be required to analyse, interpret or evaluate what you have learnt about the symptoms of schizophrenia.

4 Explain anhedonia as a symptom of schizophrenia. [2 marks] AO1 = 2

SAMPLE ANSWER: *Anhedonia is a negative symptom, characterised by the inability to experience physical pleasures such as food and bodily contact (physical anhedonia) or the inability to experience pleasure from interpersonal situations such as interacting with other people (social anhedonia).*

5 Professor Caroline Smith was interested in the ways in which DSM (*The Diagnostic and Statistical Manual of Psychiatric Disorders*) has changed its views on schizophrenia since it was introduced in 1952. She looked at all the versions up to DSM-5, which was introduced in 2013. She wrote an article on her findings and submitted it for publication in a peer-reviewed journal. Later, she wrote a book which was published in London. It was called 'How beliefs about schizophrenia have changed', and was published by *The Psychiatric Press* in 2018.

5(a)	[2 marks]	AO1 = 2
5(b)	[2 marks]	AO1 = 2
5(c)	[2 marks]	AO1 = 2
5(d)	[2 marks]	AO2 = 2

(a) Professor Smith collected secondary data in her study. Explain what is meant by 'secondary data'.

Exam tip

Be prepared for research methods questions to be asked on any of the topics you have studied!

(b) Outline the purpose of the abstract section in a scientific report.

(c) Professor Smith's article underwent a peer review process. Briefly explain **one** reason why it is important for research to undergo this process.

(d) Write the full reference for Professor Smith's book as it should appear in the reference section of another researcher's report.

Exam tip

When referencing books, a suitable format is: Author's surname, author's initial, date in brackets, title of book, place of publication, publisher.

Reliability and validity in diagnosis and classification

Specification notes
Reliability and validity in diagnosis and classification of schizophrenia, including reference to co-morbidity, culture and gender bias and symptom overlap.

Year 2 Student Book Pages 140–141

1 Which **one** of the following is the best definition of co-morbidity as the term is used in the diagnosis/classification of schizophrenia?

Tick **one** box only.

A	The consistency of diagnoses made by two independent clinicians.	
B	The occurrence of two or more symptoms in a person diagnosed as schizophrenic.	
C	The extent to which two or more people diagnosed as schizophrenic share the same symptoms.	
D	The extent to which two or more conditions occur simultaneously in a person.	

[1 mark]   AO1 = 1

2 Outline the role of culture in the diagnosis and/or classification of schizophrenia.

There is a significant variation between countries in the diagnosis of schizophrenia. For example, Copeland _____

_____

_____

Copeland found that _____

_____

_____

[3 marks]   AO1 = 3

> ⭐ **Exam tip**
>
> A cultural bias is the tendency to judge all people in terms of your own cultural assumptions, which distorts or biases your judgement.

3 Explain the difference between symptom overlap and co-morbidity in the classification and/or diagnosis of schizophrenia.

Symptom overlap is where _____

_____

For example, _____

_____

However, co-morbidity is _____

_____

For example, _____

_____

[4 marks]   AO1 = 4

> ⭐ **Exam tip**
>
> Remember that when you are asked to explain a difference between two things, you need to compare the two. Using words such as 'however' or 'whereas' will help you.

4. A researcher was interested in finding out whether there was a gender bias in the diagnosis and/or classification of schizophrenia. He showed transcripts of clinical interviews to a sample of 60 psychiatrists, asking them whether they would diagnose schizophrenia on the basis of these transcripts. One group of psychiatrists was told that all the interviews were with males, a second group was told that they were with females and a third group was told nothing about the gender of the individuals interviewed.

4(a)	[2 marks]	AO2 = 2
4(b)	[2 marks]	AO2 = 2
4(c)	[2 marks]	AO2 = 2
4(d)	[2 marks]	AO1 = 2
4(e)	[3 marks]	AO1 = 1 AO2 = 2
4(f)	[3 marks]	AO2 = 3

(a) What was the aim of this study?

(b) Outline the difference between an aim and a hypothesis.

> **Exam tip**
>
> Remember, a non-directional hypothesis does not state the direction of the predicted difference or correlation.

(c) Identify the independent and dependent variables in this study.

(d) Write a non-directional hypothesis for this study.

(e) The researcher decided to carry out a pilot study first. Briefly explain what a pilot study is and why it would be appropriate here.

(f) The researcher also wanted to assess inter-observer reliability within the three groups. Explain how he could do this.

_____

 Exam tip

Inter-observer reliability is the extent to which there is agreement between two or more observers involved in the observation of a behaviour.

---

5 Finn and Ferdi were discussing issues in the diagnosis and classification of schizophrenia. 'A diagnosis can be reliable without being valid', said Ferdi. 'No,' said Finn, 'it's the other way round. A diagnosis can be valid without being reliable.'

Distinguish between reliability and validity, and explain which of Finn or Ferdi's view is correct.

Reliability in diagnosis is _____

However, validity of diagnosis is _____

Finn's view is correct/not correct because _____

Ferdi's view is correct/not correct because _____

[4 marks] AO1 = 2 AO2 = 2

 Exam tip

Reliability refers to the consistency of measurements, whereas validity refers to whether an observed effect is a genuine one.

6 Outline and evaluate issues associated with the classification and diagnosis of schizophrenia.

[16 marks] AO1 = 6 AO3 = 10

The suggested paragraph starters below will help form your answer:

- One issue is the reliability of diagnosis. This is … (AO1)
- Another issue is the validity of diagnosis. This is … (AO1)
- Co-morbidity and symptom overlap are also issues in the classification and diagnosis of schizophrenia. Co-morbidity is … (AO1)
- Symptom overlap is … (AO1)
- There is also a cultural bias when schizophrenia is being diagnosed … (AO1)
- There is a gender bias in schizophrenia diagnosis … (AO1)
- There is research support for the idea that there are cultural differences in schizophrenia diagnosis. For example, the prognosis for members of ethnic minority groups … (AO3)
- There is also research support for gender bias in diagnosis. For example, Loring and Powell … (AO3)
- One issue with diagnosing schizophrenia is inter-observer reliability. For example, Waley found … (AO3)
- One problem with co-morbidity is that it may have negative consequences for people diagnosed with schizophrenia. For example, Weber *et al* … (AO3)
- A final problem with diagnosing schizophrenia is that it doesn't tell us very much about a person's chance of improvement … (AO3)

Exam tip

For a 16 mark question, you should aim for 5 evaluation points or 4 if you discuss them in more detail.

Biological explanations for schizophrenia

Specification notes
Biological explanations for schizophrenia: genetics, the dopamine hypothesis, and neural correlates.

Year 2
Student Book
Pages 142–143

1 Which **one** of the following best describes the dopamine hypothesis of schizophrenia?

Tick **one** box only.

[1 mark] AO1 = 1

A	The positive symptoms of schizophrenia are caused by a deficiency of dopamine in certain brain regions.	
B	An excess of dopamine is associated with both the positive and negative symptoms of schizophrenia.	
C	The positive symptoms of schizophrenia are caused by an excess of dopamine in certain brain regions.	
D	The negative symptoms of schizophrenia are caused by an excess of dopamine in certain brain regions.	

2 Outline **one or more** neural correlates associated with schizophrenia.

[4 marks] AO1 = 4

One neural correlate is damage to _____

_____

Research shows that _____

_____

Individuals with schizophrenia have _____

_____

Research also shows that _____

_____

 Exam tip

You could write about one neural correlate in detail or two neural correlates in less detail.

3 Outline **one** study that has investigated the role of genetics in schizophrenia.

[3 marks] AO1 = 3

Tienari *et al.* studied 164 adoptees whose biological mothers had been diagnosed with

schizophrenia, and 197 control adoptees whose _____

_____

_____

They found that _____

_____

This shows that _____

_____

 Exam tip

You could write about a family or twin study instead of an adoption study if you wanted to.

4 In several research studies, the concordance rates for schizophrenia have been shown to be several times higher for monozygotic than for dizygotic twins, even though twins are typically raised in the same environments.

Using your knowledge of biological explanations for schizophrenia, outline why this finding can be taken as support for the view that genetic factors play a role in schizophrenia.

Genetic explanations for schizophrenia claim that _____
_____

A concordance rate is _____
_____

If a concordance rate for monozygotic twins is higher than for dizygotic twins this means that
_____
_____

Therefore, this finding _____
_____

[4 marks] AO1 = 2 AO2 = 2

Topic link

Genetic explanations of behaviour are covered on pages 132–133 of the Year 1 Student Book.

---

5 Outline and evaluate the dopamine hypothesis as an explanation for schizophrenia.

The dopamine hypothesis states _____
_____
_____

The revised dopamine hypothesis proposes _____
_____
_____

Supporting evidence for the role of dopamine comes from the use of antipsychotics _____
_____
_____
_____
_____
_____

However, the dopamine hypothesis is challenged because of evidence that shows _____
_____
_____
_____
_____

[8 marks] AO1 = 3 AO3 = 5

6 Outline and evaluate biological explanations for schizophrenia.

[16 marks] AO1 = 6 AO3 = 10

The suggested paragraph starters below will help form your answer:

- The biological explanation for schizophrenia says that genetic factors may be involved. Twin studies have found … (AO1)
- The biological explanation also includes the dopamine hypothesis. This says that … (AO1)
- Neural correlates may play a role in the development of schizophrenia … (AO1)
- One limitation of twin studies is that a higher concordance rate may be the result of environmental, as well as genetic, factors … (AO3)
- There is research support for the dopamine hypothesis. For example, drug therapy … (AO3)
- One problem with the dopamine hypothesis is that it has been challenged. For example, Noll et al … (AO3)
- A second problem with the dopamine hypothesis is that there is inconclusive evidence for it. For example, Moncrieff … (AO3)
- There is research support for the lack of grey matter in schizophrenic patients. For example, Vita et al … (AO3)

 Exam tip

This is a very large topic, with lots of AO1 and AO3 material. You will need to think carefully about which material you would use in an exam answer, because you certainly wouldn't be able to use it all!

 Exam tip

You can evaluate the methodology used in research studies, but you will only receive credit if you make this evaluation relevant to your discussion of biological explanations for schizophrenia.

Psychological explanations for schizophrenia

Specification notes
Psychological explanations for schizophrenia: family dysfunction and cognitive explanations, including dysfunctional thought processing.

Year 2 Student Book Pages 144–145

---

1 Which **one** of the following is **not** an example of dysfunctional thought processing?

Tick **one** box only.

A	Paranoid delusions	
B	Avolition	
C	Auditory hallucinations	
D	Delusions of grandeur	

[1 mark] AO1 = 1

---

2 Outline **one** psychological explanation for schizophrenia.

Cognitive explanations of schizophrenia say that the disorder develops as a result of _____
_____
_____

For example _____
_____

This can explain some symptoms, such as hallucinations and delusions, by _____
_____
_____

[4 marks] AO1 = 4

> **Exam tip**
> You could, of course, write about family dysfunction instead of cognitive explanations.

---

3 A researcher was interested in the role that families play in schizophrenia. She believed that in families where there is high expressed emotion, schizophrenics would be significantly more likely to relapse than would be the case in families where there is low expressed emotion. She decided to conduct an observational study of ten families in which one person was schizophrenic, and recorded her observations using event sampling.

3(a) [2 marks] AO1 = 2
3(b) [1 mark] AO1 = 1
3(c) [2 marks] AO2 = 2

(a) Outline what is involved in event sampling.

_____
_____
_____
_____

(b) Name an alternative procedure to event sampling which can be used in observational studies.

_____
_____

(c) Suggest **two** behavioural categories the researcher could use to record expressed emotion during her observations.

_____

> **Topic link**
> You can find out more about observational design on pages 200–201 of the Year 1 Student Book.

	3(d)	[1 mark]	AO2 = 1
	3(e)	[1 mark]	AO1 = 1

(d) The researcher counted the number of observations for each of the categories she used. Name the level of measurement in her study.

_____

_____

(e) Identify **one** statistical test that can be used to analyse data at the level of measurement you identified in **question (d)**.

_____

_____

[8 marks]	AO1 = 4	AO3 = 4

4 Outline and evaluate family dysfunction as an explanation for schizophrenia.

Double bind theory says that children who receive contradictory messages from their parents are

_____

_____

_____

For example, _____

_____

_____

This experience leads to _____

_____

_____

Expressed emotion is a family communication style which is characterised by _____

_____

_____

There is research support for the idea that family relationships are involved in the development of schizophrenia. For example, Tienari *et al* _____

_____

_____

_____

One strength of double bind theory is that there is research support for it. For example, _____

_____

_____

_____

> ★ **Exam tip**
>
> On a question like this, you can use a 'depth' approach and write about one explanation in detail, or a 'breadth' approach and write about two or more explanations in less detail.

One limitation of the expressed emotion explanation is that schizophrenics differ in their vulnerability to the influence of high expressed emotion. For example, Altorfer *et al* _____

_____

_____

_____

5 Outline and evaluate psychological explanations for schizophrenia.

[16 marks] AO1 = 6 AO3 = 10

The suggested paragraph starters below will help form your answer:

- One psychological explanation of schizophrenia is double bind theory. This says that schizophrenia develops as a result of … (AO1)
- Another psychological explanation of schizophrenia is expressed emotion … (AO1)
- Cognitive explanations claim that schizophrenia is a result of dysfunctional thought processing … (AO1)
- One limitation of the double bind theory is that the evidence for it is, at best, mixed. For example,… (AO3)
- One limitation of the expressed emotional explanation is that schizophrenics differ in their vulnerability to the influence of high expressed emotion . For example, Altorfer *et al* … (AO3)
- An issue with psychological explanations of schizophrenia is that family relationships may interact with genetic factors … (AO3)
- One strength of explaining schizophrenia in terms of dysfunctional thought processing is that it can explain both the positive and negative symptoms … (AO3)
- Another strength of cognitive explanations of schizophrenia is that findings related to CBTp support them. For example, NICE … (AO3)

Exam tip

Note this asks for explanations (plural) so, if you only write about one explanation, then you are showing 'partial performance', and this will limit the credit you can be given for your answer.

Exam tip

You must remember to evaluate each of the explanations you have outlined.

Drug therapy

Specification notes
Drug therapy: typical and atypical antipsychotics.

Year 2
Student Book
Pages 146–147

---

1 Which **one** of the following is an accurate statement of how typical antipsychotic drugs treat schizophrenia?

Tick **one** box only.

[1 mark] AO1 = 1

A	Typical antipsychotics cause an increase in dopamine's effects.	
B	Typical antipsychotics cause a reduction in dopamine's effects.	
C	Typical antipsychotics cause an increase in dopamine's and serotonin's effects.	
D	Typical antipsychotics cause a reduction in dopamine's and serotonin's effects.	

---

2 Evaluate the use of antipsychotic drugs as a therapy for schizophrenia.

[4 marks] AO3 = 4

One limitation of drug therapy is that drugs have side effects. For example, typical antipsychotics can cause _____

_____

If patients keep using them then _____

_____

_____

This means that _____

_____

> ⭐ **Exam tip**
>
> As there are only 4 marks available, you can choose to make one evaluation point in detail, or two evaluation points in less detail.

---

3 Researchers carried out a study of the effectiveness of antipsychotics in the treatment of schizophrenia. They advertised in the psychiatric ward of a local hospital, asking for volunteers to take part in the study. This led to a sample of 32 individuals who were being treated using antipsychotics. Half of these individuals continued to take their regular dosage of the antipsychotic for three months, whereas the other half were given a placebo. At the end of the study, both groups were assessed by a psychiatrist for the severity of their symptoms.

(a) Write a suitable directional hypothesis for this study.

3(a) [3 marks] AO2 = 3

> ⭐ **Exam tip**
>
> Remember, a directional hypothesis states the direction of the predicted difference or correlation.

(b) What type of sample was used in this study? Give **one** limitation of this method of sampling.

_____
_____
_____
_____
_____
_____

(c) Outline **one** way in which the researchers could have minimised the risk of bias when allocating individuals to either the antipsychotic or placebo group.

_____
_____
_____
_____

(d) What is meant by investigator effects? Explain why investigator effects might have been an issue in this study.

_____
_____
_____
_____
_____
_____
_____

(e) Outline **one** ethical issue that might have arisen in this study.

_____
_____
_____
_____

3(b)	[3 marks]	AO2 = 1	AO3 = 2
3(c)	[2 marks]	AO2 = 2	
3(d)	[4 marks]	AO1 = 2	AO2 = 2
3(e)	[2 marks]	AO2 = 2	

> ★ **Exam tip**
>
> Make sure the ethical issue you outline is relevant to the study described in the stimulus material.

4 Matt is a schizophrenic who rarely talks and typically lies in his bed for much of the day. His medical records show that he has been receiving typical antipsychotic treatment for years. A clinician believes that Matt might benefit from treatment using an atypical antipsychotic, and suggests a change to Matt's medication.

[4 marks] AO2 = 4

Use your knowledge of drug therapy for schizophrenia to explain why the clinician might have suggested a change to Matt's medication.

Typical antipsychotic drugs work by _____

_____

Unfortunately, one side effect of the drugs Matt is taking is _____

_____

One strength of atypical antipsychotic drugs Matt's clinician wants him to change to is _____

_____

This means that _____

_____

> **Exam tip**
>
> Remember that you are being asked to apply your knowledge of drug therapy to 'Matt', so don't write a general answer to this question.

5 Outline the use of atypical antipsychotics in the treatment of schizophrenia and give **one** strength of this type of treatment.

[6 marks] AO1 = 3 AO3 = 3

Atypical antipsychotics aim to _____

_____

_____

They do this by _____

_____

_____

A strength of this type of treatment is that _____

_____

_____

For example, they are less likely to experience _____

_____

_____

This means _____

_____

_____

> **Exam tip**
>
> Always read exam questions carefully. This one is about a strength of atypical antipsychotics, so you will not get any marks if you write about typical antipsychotics.

6 Outline and evaluate drug therapy as a treatment for schizophrenia. [16 marks] AO1 = 6, AO3 = 10

The suggested paragraph starters below will help form your answer:

- Typical antipsychotics aim to reduce dopamine. They do this by … (AO1)
- Atypical antipsychotics also aim to reduce dopamine. They do this by … (AO1)
- One strength of antipsychotics is that they are effective in treating schizophrenia. For example, Leucht *et al*. found … (AO3)
- However, one weakness of typical antipsychotics is the side effects they produce … (AO3)
- However, while atypical antipsychotics have fewer side effects, they do not seem to be more effective than typical antipsychotics. For example, Crossley *et al* found … (AO3)
- An important point about drug therapy in general is that it raises several ethical issues. For example … (AO3)

> **Exam tip**
> You can evaluate drug therapy by comparing it with other therapies, such as family therapy.

> **Exam tip**
> One way to evaluate any form of therapy is to play your **ACES**. This involves writing about:
> - **A**ppropriateness of the therapy
> - **C**oncept of cure
> - **E**ffectiveness
> - **S**ide effects
>
> You could write about ethical issues as a fifth evaluation point, if you needed to.

Cognitive behavioural therapy

Specification notes
Cognitive behaviour therapy as used in the treatment of schizophrenia.

Year 2
Student Book
Pages 148–149

1. Which **one** of the following statements is **true** about cognitive behavioural therapy as a treatment for schizophrenia?

   Tick **one** box only.

A	Cognitive behavioural therapy is never used with other therapies in the treatment of schizophrenia.	
B	Cognitive behavioural therapy can only be used as part of group therapy.	
C	Cognitive behavioural therapy only focuses on the negative symptoms of schizophrenia.	
D	Cognitive behavioural therapy aims to change the maladaptive thoughts and beliefs that occur in schizophrenia.	

   [1 mark]   AO1 = 1

    Topic link

   CBT is also used as a therapy for depression. See pages 110–111 of the Year 1 Student Book.

2. Explain how cognitive behavioural therapy can be used as a way to treat schizophrenia.

   CBTp focuses on _____

   _____

   _____

   It does this by disputing irrational thoughts and beliefs. For example _____

   _____

   _____

   Clients might be encouraged to _____

   _____

   _____

   During CBTp, the therapist _____

   _____

   _____

   [6 marks]   AO1 = 6

    Exam tip

   Notice the word 'how' and do not waste time writing unnecessary detail about *why* the therapy might be used to treat schizophrenia.

3. In a study looking at the effectiveness of cognitive behavioural therapy, a researcher investigated the relationship between how many 'behavioural assignments' a therapist set a schizophrenic during treatment and the therapist's rating of the schizophrenic's general level of functioning. The researcher predicted that there would be a positive correlation between the number of assignments and the general level of functioning. Ten therapists and ten schizophrenics were studied, and a correlation of +0.449 was found.

   (a) Was the researcher's hypothesis directional or non-directional? Explain your answer.

   _____

   _____

   _____

   3(a)   [2 marks]   AO2 = 2

(b) The researcher reported a positive correlation between the two variables. Explain the difference between a positive and a negative correlation.

_____

_____

_____

_____

(c) Suggest **one** way in which the researcher might have displayed this correlation in graphical form.

_____

_____

(d) The researcher's data is quantitative. What is meant by quantitative data, and how does this differ from qualitative data?

_____

_____

_____

_____

_____

_____

(e) The researcher decided to analyse her data using a Spearman's rho test. Using the information in the table below, state whether or not the correlation is significant at the 0.05 level of significance. Justify your answer.

Level of significance for a two-tailed test	0.10	0.05
Level of significance for a one-tailed test	0.05	0.025
N = 10	0.564	0.648
N = 20	0.380	0.447

The calculated value must be EQUAL TO or GREATER THAN the tabled value for significance at the level shown.

_____

_____

_____

_____

_____

_____

3(b)	[2 marks]	AO1 = 2
3(c)	[1 mark]	AO2 = 1
3(d)	[3 marks]	AO1 = 3
3(e)	[3 marks]	AO2 = 3

Topic link

You can read more about Correlations on pages 206–207 of the Year 1 Student Book.

Topic link

You can read about the Spearman's rho test on page 30 of the Year 2 Student Book.

Exam tip

The 'calculated value' is the value obtained when the test is used. The 'tabled' (or 'critical') value is the value it is compared with in order to make a decision about statistical significance.

4 Discuss the use of cognitive behavioural therapy as a therapy for schizophrenia.

[16 marks] AO1 = 6 AO3 = 10

The suggested paragraph starters below will help form your answer:

- Cognitive behavioural therapy for schizophrenia (CBTp) aims to … (AO1)
- CBTp has various phases, including … (AO1)
- For example, clients might be asked to … (AO1)
- One limitation with CBTp as a therapy for schizophrenia is that is difficult to assess how effective it is. For example … (AO3)
- A second limitation of CBTp is that its appropriateness and effectiveness seems to depend on the stage of a schizophrenic's disorder … (AO3)
- A third limitation is that there are methodological problems with some meta-analytic studies into CBTp's effectiveness … (AO3)
- A fourth limitation is that methodologically sound meta-analyses of CBTp's effectiveness suggest it has little therapeutic benefit … (AO3)
- A final limitation with CBTp is that it is not yet an established therapy in the treatment of schizophrenia … (AO3)

 Exam tip

You need to make sure that all your AO1 and AO3 points are related to how CBTp is used specifically in the treatment of schizophrenia rather than discuss CBT as a general approach to treatment.

Exam tip

You could also play your **ACES** on this question, and/or make comparisons with other types of therapy.
- **A**ppropriateness of the therapy
- **C**oncept of cure
- **E**ffectiveness
- **S**ide effects

Family therapy

Specification notes
Family therapy as used in the treatment of schizophrenia.

Year 2
Student Book
Pages 150–151

1 Which **one** of the following is a feature of family therapy as it is used in the treatment of schizophrenia?

Tick **one** box only.

[1 mark] AO1 = 1

A	Using strategies to decrease expressed emotions by family members.	
B	Encouraging the schizophrenic to listen to complaints from family members.	
C	Using daily reports from family members to make judgements about the schizophrenic.	
D	Using strategies to increase expressed emotions by family members.	

2 Evaluate family therapy as a way to treat schizophrenia.

[4 marks] AO3 = 4

One strength of family therapy is _____

_____

For example, the NICE review found _____

_____

The initial cost is offset _____

_____

This means that _____

_____

> ⭐ **Exam tip**
>
> As there are only 4 marks available, you can choose to make one evaluation point in detail, or two evaluation points in less detail.

3 A meta-analysis of studies of family therapy concluded that family therapy is effective in improving clinical outcomes for individuals with schizophrenia. This led to the claim that family therapy has considerable economic benefits associated with the treatment of schizophrenia.

3 (a) [2 marks] AO1 = 2
3 (b) [4 marks] AO3 = 4

(a) What is meant by a 'meta-analysis'?

_____

_____

_____

_____

(b) Give **one** strength and **one** limitation of meta-analysis.

_____
_____
_____
_____
_____
_____
_____

(c) A problem with the meta-analysis described in the item is that many of the studies used lacked random allocation to the family therapy or control conditions. What is meant by random allocation, and why is the lack of this an issue in meta-analysis?

_____
_____
_____
_____
_____
_____
_____
_____
_____
_____

(d) Explain how the findings of this meta-analysis might have implications for the economy.

_____
_____
_____
_____
_____
_____
_____

3(c)	[4 marks]	AO1 = 2	AO3 = 2
3(d)	[3 marks]	AO2 = 3	

> ⭐ **Exam tip**
>
> Avoid saying 'random allocation is where participants are allocated randomly'!

> ⭐ **Exam tip**
>
> Think about whether the findings might cost or save tax payers money.

4 A researcher wanted to study family therapy and drug therapy as treatments for schizophrenia. He looked at the therapies in terms of how successful they were in reducing symptoms and how costly they were to health providers. He judged drug therapy to be more effective in terms of behaviour change, but family therapy to be more effective in terms of cost.

Outline **one** other factor the researcher could have used to compare family therapy and drug therapy, and suggest a conclusion that he might have drawn.

One factor is _____

_____

For example, family therapy _____

_____

However, with drug therapy _____

_____

This suggests that _____

_____

[4 marks] AO2 = 4

 Exam tip

There are several comparisons that could be made between the two therapies, such as side effects, ethical issues, or appropriateness.

5 Outline family therapy as a way to treat schizophrenia and give **one** limitation of this treatment method.

Family therapy aims to _____

_____

_____

It does this by _____

_____

One limitation of family therapy is that _____

_____

For example, Garety *et al* found no difference between _____

_____

Garety *et al.* concluded that _____

_____

_____

[6 marks] AO1 = 3 AO3 = 3

 Exam tip

Remember that a limitation is a 'weakness', so writing about a strength of family therapy will not receive credit.

6 Outline and evaluate family therapy as a way of treating schizophrenia. [16 marks] AO1 = 6 AO3 = 10

The suggested paragraph starters below will help form your answer:

- Family therapy aims to … (AO1)
- It does this by … (AO1)
- Family therapy also provides family members with … (AO1)
- One strength of family therapy is that it has been shown to have a positive impact on family members, as well as on the person with schizophrenia … (AO3)
- Another strength of family therapy is that it has economic benefits … (AO3)
- However, one limitation of family therapy is that there are methodological issues in studies investigating its effectiveness … (AO3)
- A second limitation of family therapy is that carers low in expressed emotion might be just as effective … (AO3)
- A final limitation of family therapy is that its only benefit may be that it increases medication compliance … (AO3)

> **Exam tip**
>
> You could also evaluate family therapy by comparing it with other therapies, such as drug therapy, or by playing your ACES as we've suggested with other therapies..

Token economy and the management of schizophrenia

Specification notes
Token economies as used in the management of schizophrenia.

Year 2
Student Book
Pages 152–153

① Which **one** of the following statements about token economies is **true**?

Tick **one** box only.

A	There are no ethical issues associated with token economies.	
B	Token economies lead to permanent behavioural changes.	
C	Token economies use negative reinforcement to change behaviour.	
D	Token economies use both primary and secondary reinforcers.	

[1 mark]   AO1 = 1

Exam tip

You will have studied the behavioural approach to explaining and treating phobias in the Psychopathology unit of your course, and could use some of that knowledge here.

② Explain **one** limitation of token economies as a way to manage schizophrenia.

One limitation of token economies is _____

_____

For example, Corrigan argues that _____

_____

In a psychiatric setting _____

_____

However, outpatients _____

_____

This means that _____

_____

[4 marks]   AO3 = 4

Exam tip

You have only been asked to write about one limitation, so don't do more than you have been asked to.

③ In a study looking at the effectiveness of token economies, researchers asked two independent observers to record the activity levels of twelve chronic schizophrenics on a hospital ward. Measurements were taken before the token economy programme was implemented and six months after its implementation. The researchers found an increase in activity levels which was significant at $p<0.05$.

(a) Identify the sampling method used by the researchers.

_____

_____

(b) Explain **one** disadvantage of the sampling method you identified in **question (a)**.

_____

_____

_____

_____

3 (a) [1 mark] AO2 = 1
3 (b) [2 marks] AO3 = 2

(c) Explain **one** way in which the researchers could have recorded the behavioural categories associated with 'activity levels'.

3(c) [2 marks] AO2 = 2
3(d) [4 marks] AO2 = 4
3(e) [2 marks] AO1 = 2

_____
_____
_____
_____

(d) Explain **one** way in which the researchers could have assessed how reliable the observers were.

> ★ **Exam tip**
>
> Remember that reliability refers to the consistency of measurements, whereas validity refers to whether an observed effect is a genuine one.

_____
_____
_____
_____
_____
_____
_____
_____

(e) The researchers found that the increase in activity levels was significant at p<0.05. What is meant by 'significant at p<0.05'?

_____
_____
_____
_____

[6 marks] AO1 = 3 AO3 = 3

4 Outline the token economy as used in the management of schizophrenia and give **one** strength of this method of treatment.

The token economy system aims to _____
_____

It works by _____
_____

One strength of the token economy is _____
_____
_____

For example, Dickerson et al. found _____
_____
_____

The researchers concluded _____
_____

5 Outline and evaluate the token economy as a way of managing schizophrenia.

[16 marks] AO1 = 6 AO3 = 10

The suggested paragraph starters below will help form your answer:

- The token economy system is based on … (AO1)
- It aims to … (AO1)
- It involves … (AO1)
- One strength of the token economy is that it seems to be effective in managing schizophrenic behaviour … (AO3)
- One weakness of the token economy is that tokens may not be the reason for behaviour improvements … (AO3)
- A second weakness is that there are ethical issues about using the token economy … (AO3)
- A third weakness is that the token economy may not be effective in all settings … (AO3)
- A final weakness of token economies is that they have fallen out of use … (AO3)

> **Exam tip**
>
> You can also evaluate token economy by comparing it with other therapies, such as family therapy, or by playing your **ACES** as we've suggested with other therapies.

An interactionist approach

Specification notes
The importance of an interactionist approach in explaining and treating schizophrenia; the diathesis-stress model.

Year 2
Student Book
Pages 154–155

[1 mark] AO1 = 1

1 Which **one** of the following statements about the diathesis-stress model is **true**?

Tick **one** box only.

A	People who have a high biological vulnerability to schizophrenia always develop the disorder irrespective of stress factors.	
B	People who have a low biological vulnerability to schizophrenia never develop the disorder irrespective of stress factors.	
C	People with a high biological vulnerability to schizophrenia are less likely to develop the disorder when they experience increases in stress.	
D	People with a low biological vulnerability to schizophrenia are more likely to develop the disorder when they experience increases in stress.	

[4 marks] AO1 = 4

2 Explain the diathesis-stress model of schizophrenia.

The diathesis-stress model says that schizophrenia is the result of _____

_____

A diathesis is _____

_____

Stress is _____

_____

A combination of _____

_____

> **Exam tip**
>
> The diathesis-stress model is named on the specification, so make sure you can explain it clearly.

[4 marks] AO1 = 4

3 Outline **one** study that has explored the diathesis-stress model of schizophrenia.

Tienari *et al.* reviewed hospital records for women admitted to psychiatric hospitals and _____

_____

_____

_____

They found _____

_____

_____

_____

> **Exam tip**
>
> For full marks on this question, you need to include how the researchers carried out the study and what they found.

41

4 James was reading a book about the causes of schizophrenia. The book claimed that genetic factors are involved in schizophrenia. 'It can't be genetic,' he thought, 'because, if it was, people who have a family history of it would always develop it.'

Use your knowledge of the diathesis-stress model to explain to James why people with a genetic vulnerability to schizophrenia do not always develop the disorder.

James is wrong to think that _____

_____

This is because the diathesis-stress model states that _____

_____

However, if there are no stressors to trigger this vulnerability, then _____

_____

This would explain why _____

_____

[4 marks] AO1 = 2 AO2 = 2

> ⭐ **Exam tip**
>
> A diagram showing the relationship between biological vulnerability and stress might be helpful on this question.

5 Discuss the diathesis-stress model of schizophrenia.

[16 marks] AO1 = 6 AO3 = 10

The suggested paragraph starters below will help form your answer:

- The diathesis-stress model says that schizophrenia is the result of … (AO1)
- A diathesis is … and a stressor is … (AO1)
- People with a family history of schizophrenia … (AO1)
- However, people with a low genetic vulnerability… (AO1)
- One strength of the diathesis-stress model is that knowledge of different diatheses may help to prevent schizophrenia … (AO3)
- One strength of the diathesis-stress model is that there is research support for it. For example, Tienari et al… (AO3)
- One limitation of the diathesis-stress model is that urban environments are not necessarily more stressful … (AO3)
- A second limitation of the diathesis stress model is that genetic vulnerability is not the only diathesis that increases the risk of developing schizophrenia … (AO3)
- A third limitation of the diathesis-stress model is that determining causal stress is difficult … (AO3)

> ⭐ **Exam tip**
>
> This extended writing question would really benefit from careful planning. There is a lot of material about biological explanations (see pages 142–143 of the Year 2 Student Book) that could be used, but you will need to think carefully about what to use and what to leave out.

Exam tip

To maximise marks in extended writing questions, you need to go beyond merely identifying a critical point. You could, for example, provide supporting evidence for the point and say how this impacts on the diathesis-stress model of schizophrenia.

Notes

UNIVERSITY PRESS

Great Clarendon Street, Oxford, OX2 6DP, United Kingdom

Oxford University Press is a department of the University of Oxford. It furthers the University's objective of excellence in research, scholarship, and education by publishing worldwide. Oxford is a registered trade mark of Oxford University Press in the UK and in certain other countries.

© Oxford University Press 2018

The moral rights of the authors have been asserted

First published in 2018

All rights reserved. No part of this publication may be reproduced, stored in a retrieval system, or transmitted, in any form or by any means, without the prior permission in writing of Oxford University Press, or as expressly permitted by law, by licence or under terms agreed with the appropriate reprographics rights organization. Enquiries concerning reproduction outside the scope of the above should be sent to the Rights Department, Oxford University Press, at the address above.

You must not circulate this work in any other form and you must impose this same condition on any acquirer.

British Library Cataloguing in Publication Data
Data available

978-0-19-842896-1

5 7 9 10 8 6

Paper used in the production of this book is a natural, recyclable product made from wood grown in sustainable forests. The manufacturing process conforms to the environmental regulations of the country of origin.

Printed in Great Britain by Ashford Colour Ltd.

Acknowledgements

The publishers would like to thank the following for permissions to use their photographs:

Cover: Eric Isselee/Shutterstock

Photos: p31: Fabian Faber/Shutterstock; **p27:** Halfpoint/Shutterstock; **p12:** Erik Lam/Shutterstock; **p22:** MirasWonderland/Shutterstock; **p40:** Aneta Jungerova/Shutterstock; **p18:** Mila Atkovska/Shutterstock; **p36:** cynoclub/Shutterstock

Although we have made every effort to trace and contact all copyright holders before publication this has not been possible in all cases. If notified, the publisher will rectify any errors or omissions at the earliest opportunity.

The publishers would like to provide special thanks to the mental health charity Mind for their input and guidance when selecting the cover image for this exam workbook.

The manufacturer's authorised representative in the EU for product safety is Oxford University Press España S.A. of El Parque Empresarial San Fernando de Henares, Avenida de Castilla, 2 – 28830 Madrid (www.oup.es/en or product.safety@oup.com). OUP España S.A. also acts as importer into Spain of products made by the manufacturer.

The Complete Companions
Psychology A Level Paper 3

Authors
Clare Compton, Rob McIlveen

Series Editor
Mike Cardwell

From the team that brought you the best-selling and trusted **The Complete Companions**, **The Complete Companions Exam Workbooks** provide students with skills-building activities and step-by-step exam-style practice questions to ensure they approach their exams confident of success. They are completely matched to AQA's AS and A Level examination requirements and ideal for use in class or for homework and revision.

This **A Level Paper 3 Exam Workbook** covers **Schizophrenia**, one of the optional topics examined by A Level Paper 3.

- Complete match to both the popular *The Complete Companions* series and the specification, so you can trust that you've covered everything you need to practise.
- Written with reference to the **latest examiner reports**, so you can be confident that it reflects exactly what is required for success at A Level.
- Focussed **exam advice and tips** throughout, with suggested **AO1/AO2/AO3 mark allocations** to help structure answers.

Also available:

Paper 1 Exam Workbook for AQA
978-019-842890-9

Paper 2 Exam Workbook for AQA
978-019-842891-6

Paper 3 Exam Workbook for AQA: Relationships including Issues and debates
978-019-842895-4

Paper 3 Exam Workbook for AQA: Gender including Issues and debates
978-019-842894-7

Paper 3 Exam Workbook for AQA: Aggression
978-019-842892-3

Paper 3 Exam Workbook for AQA: Forensic psychology
978-019-842893-0

Two pages of exam questions per topic, ramped from lower tariff to essay style

Marks clearly presented with suggested breakdown of Assessment Objectives

Tips and guidance based on the latest assessment information

Essential for A Level students, with guidance to help deliver the greater depth required to achieve top grades

Answers can be found at www.oxfordsecondary.co.uk/completecompanionsanswers

OXFORD
UNIVERSITY PRESS

How to get in touch:
web   www.oxfordsecondary.co.uk
email schools.enquiries.uk@oup.com
tel   01536 452620
fax   01865 313472

ISBN 978-0-19-842896-1